Enjoy!!!

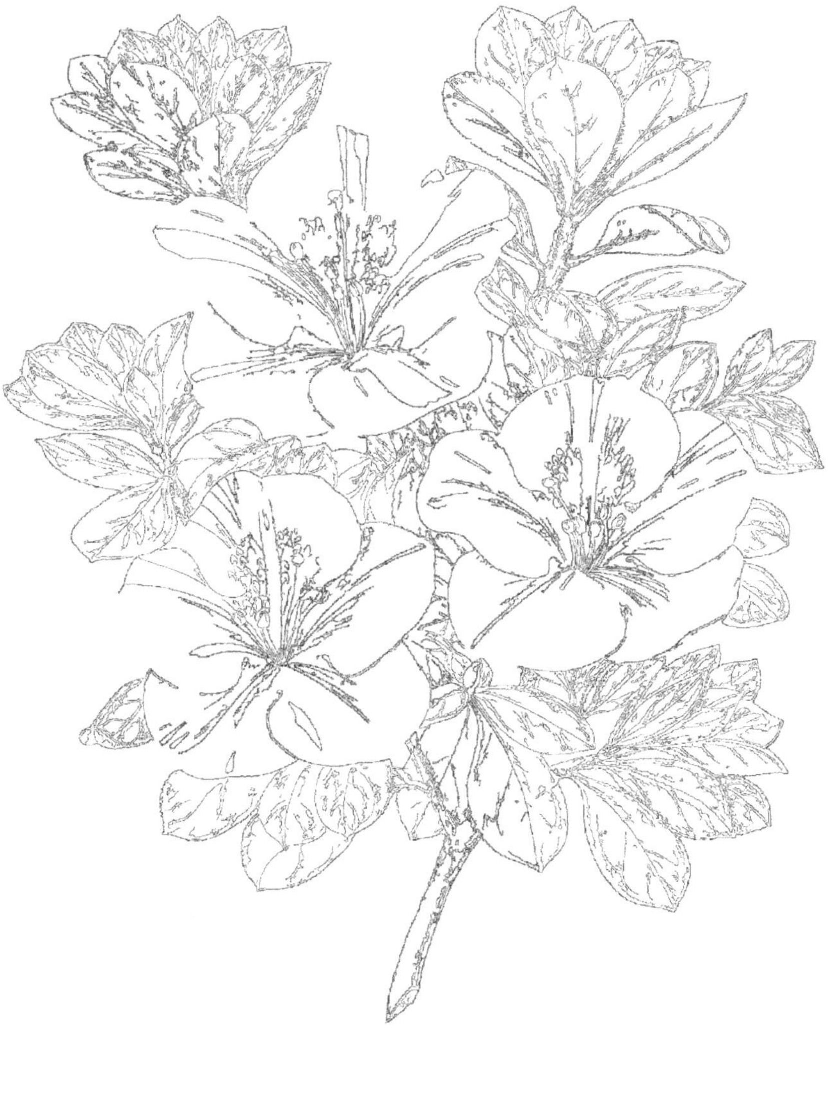

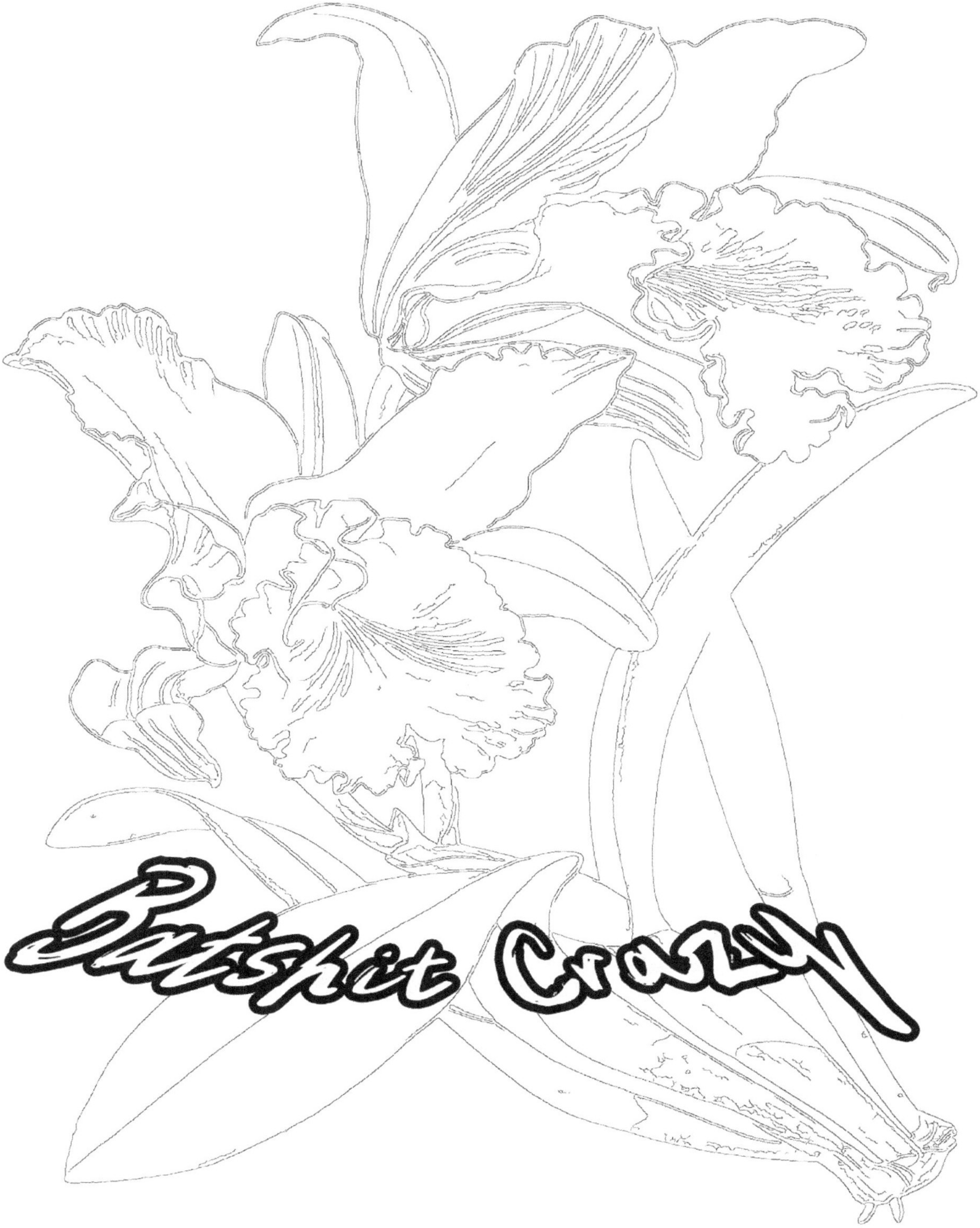
Batshit Crazy

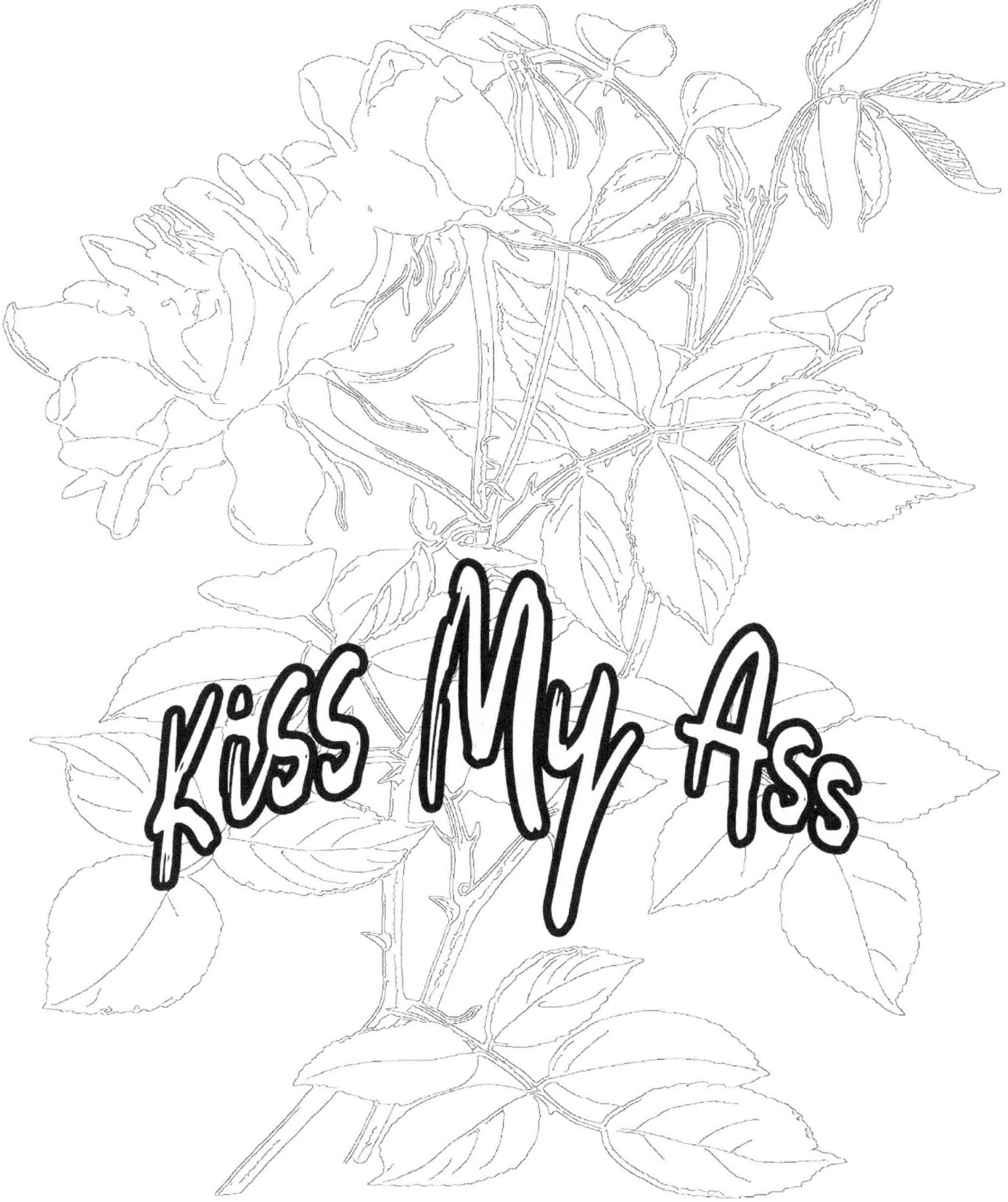
Kiss My Ass

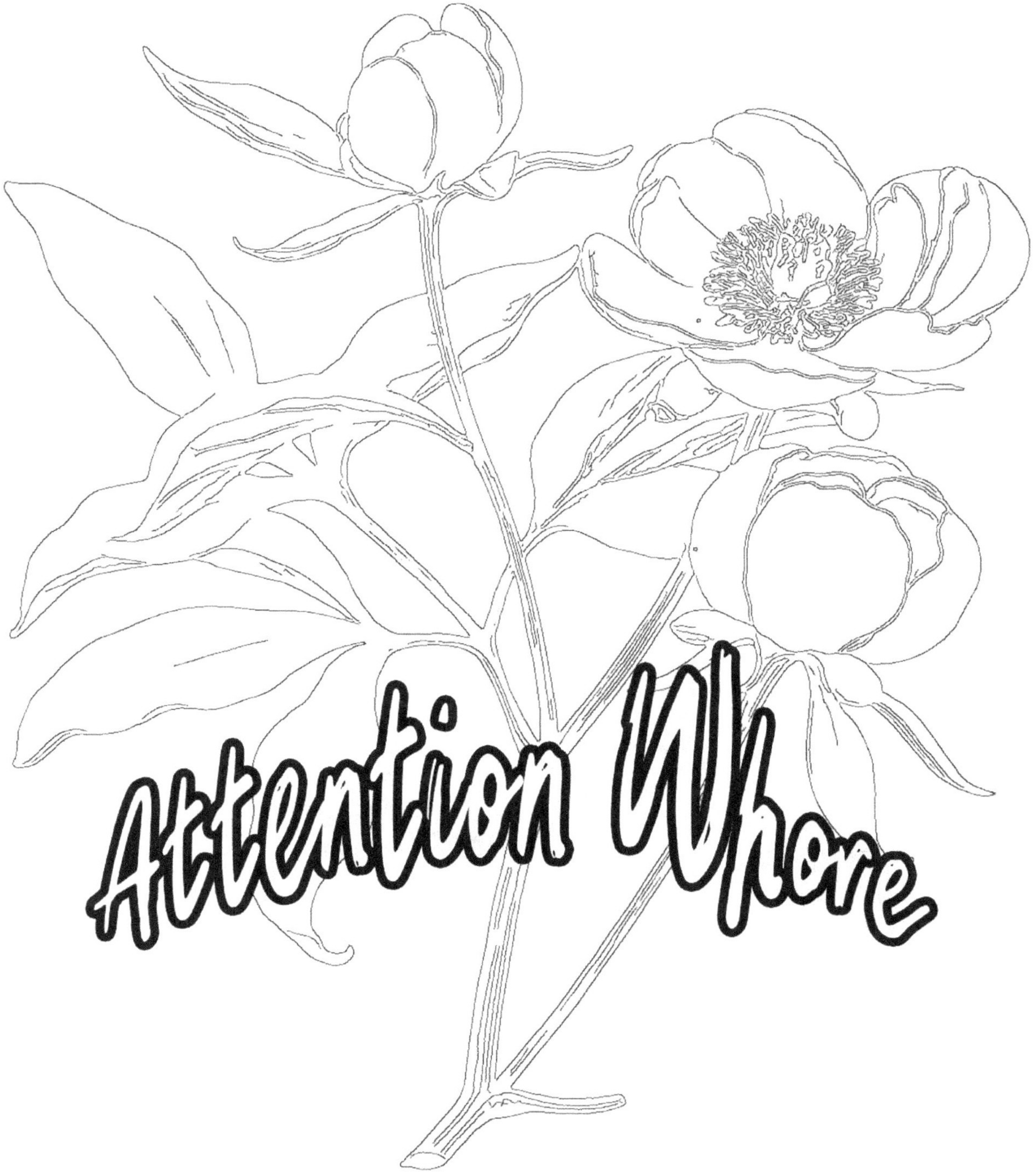
Attention Whore

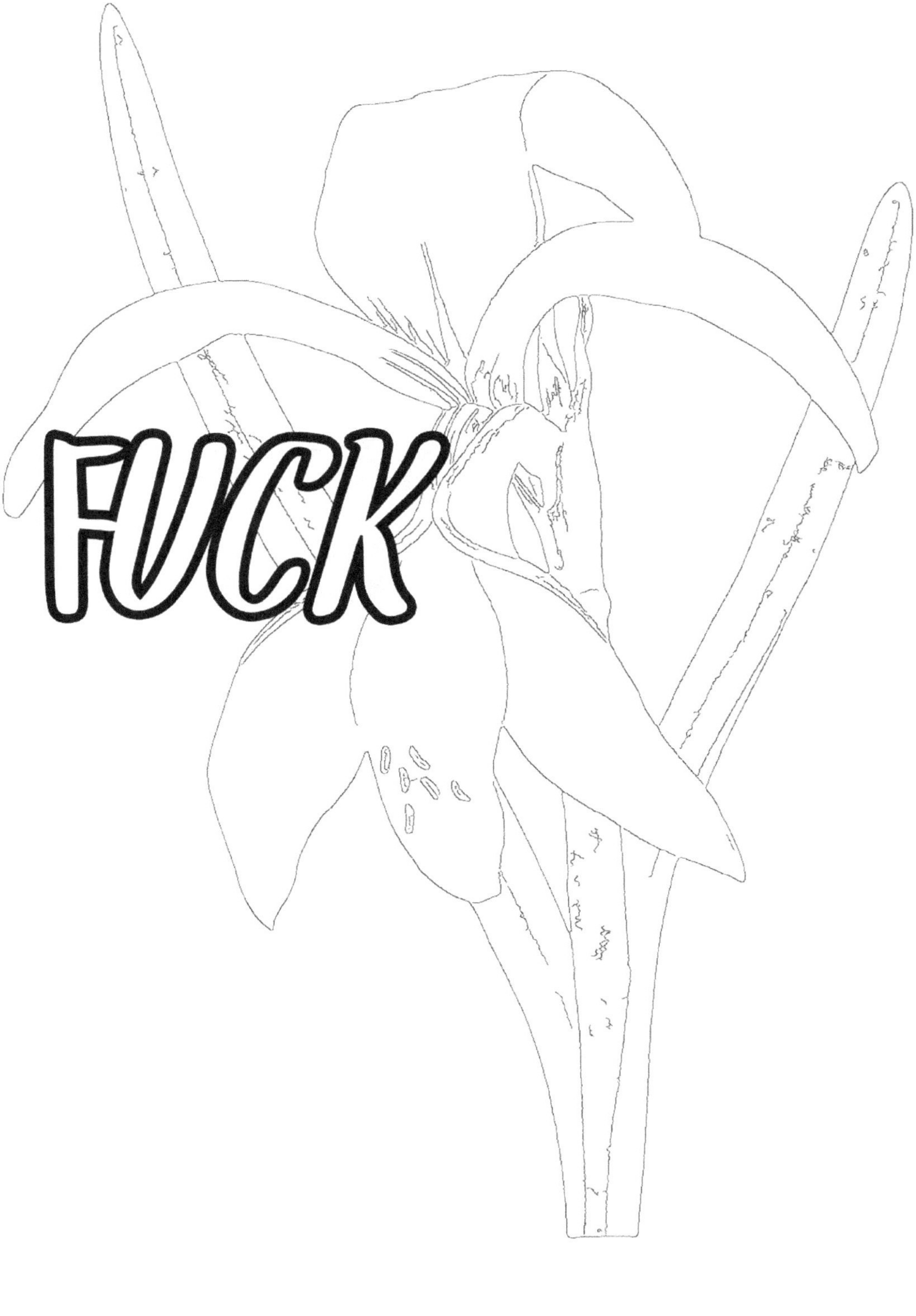
FUCK

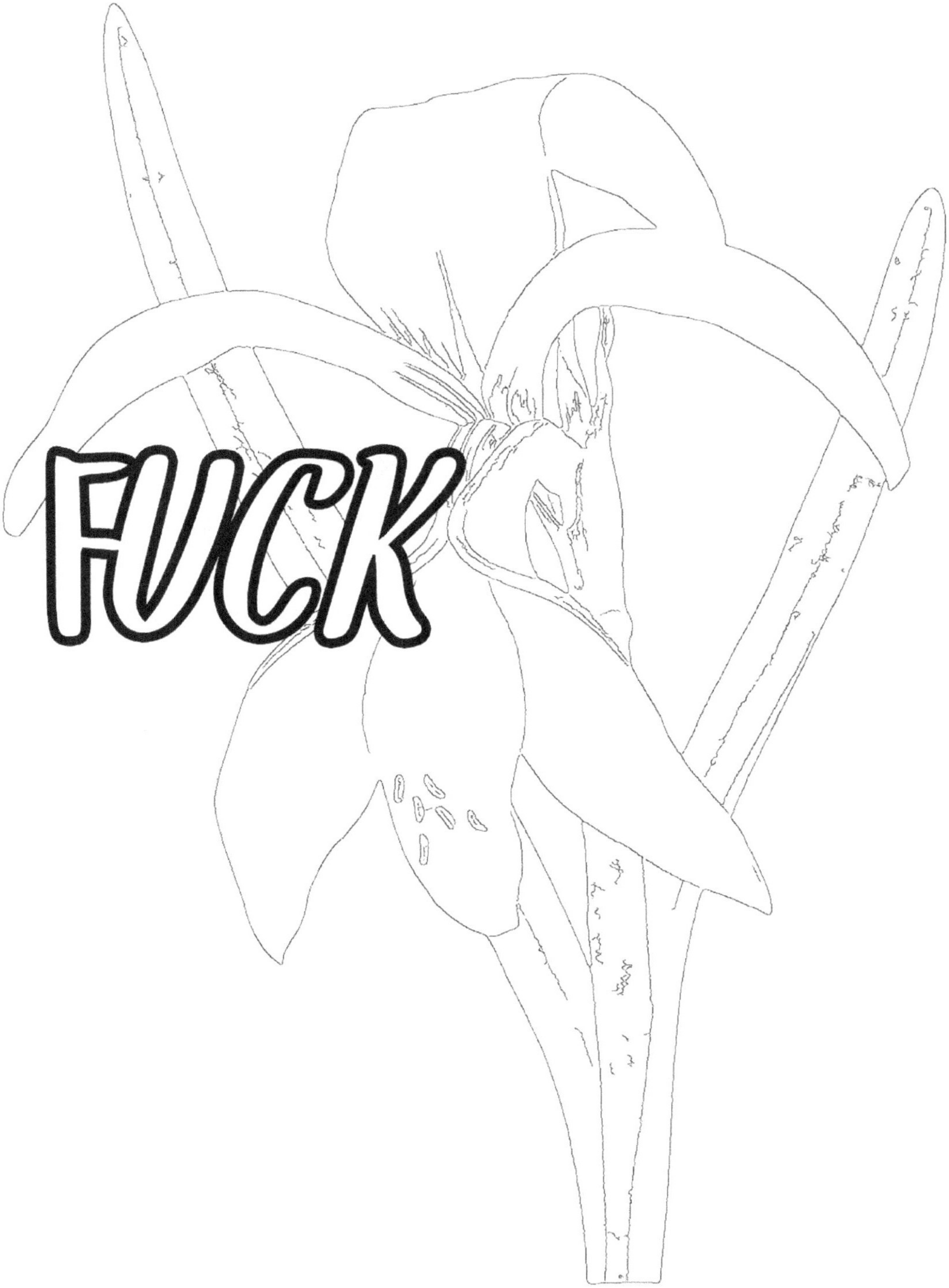
FUCK

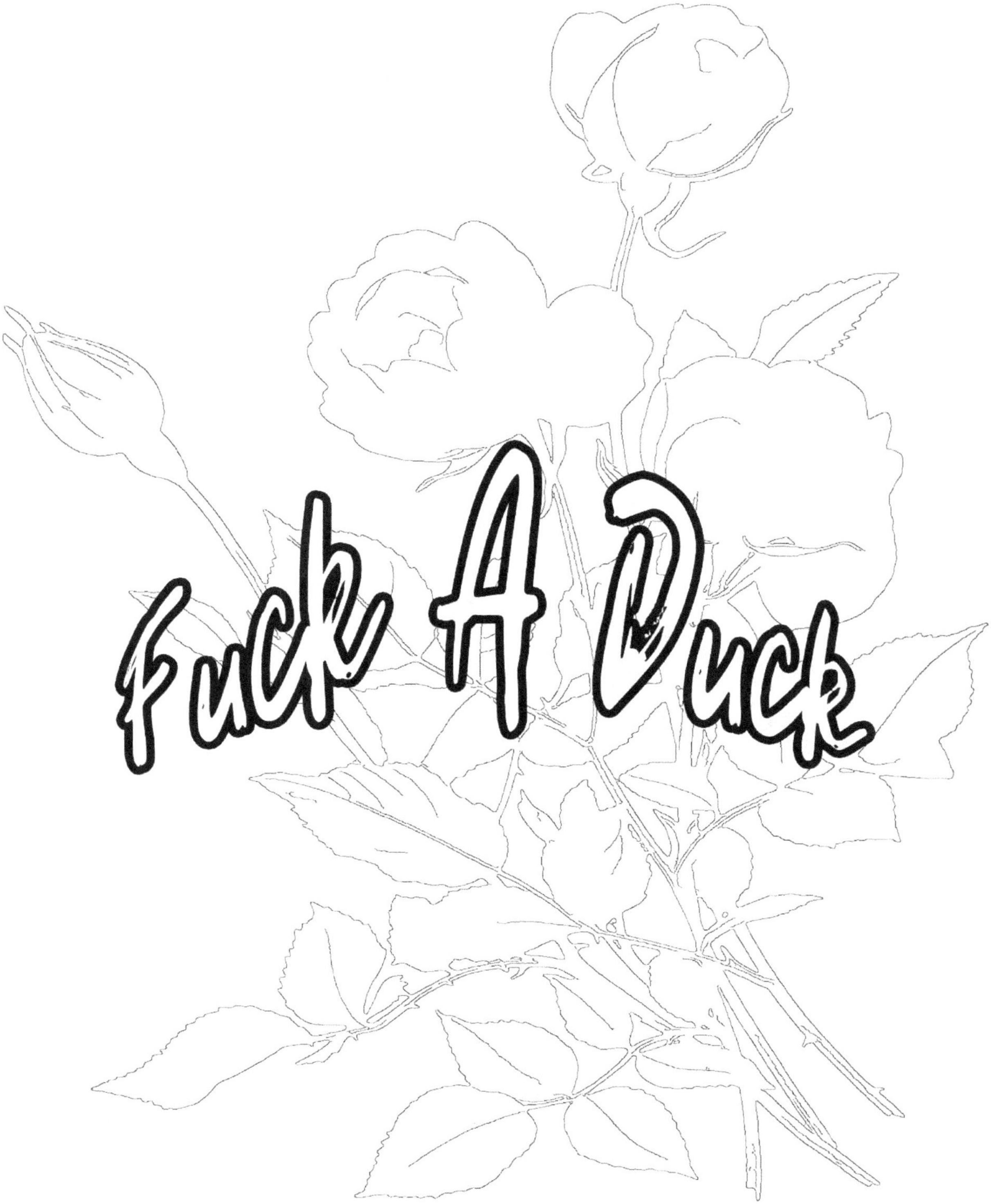
Fuck A Duck

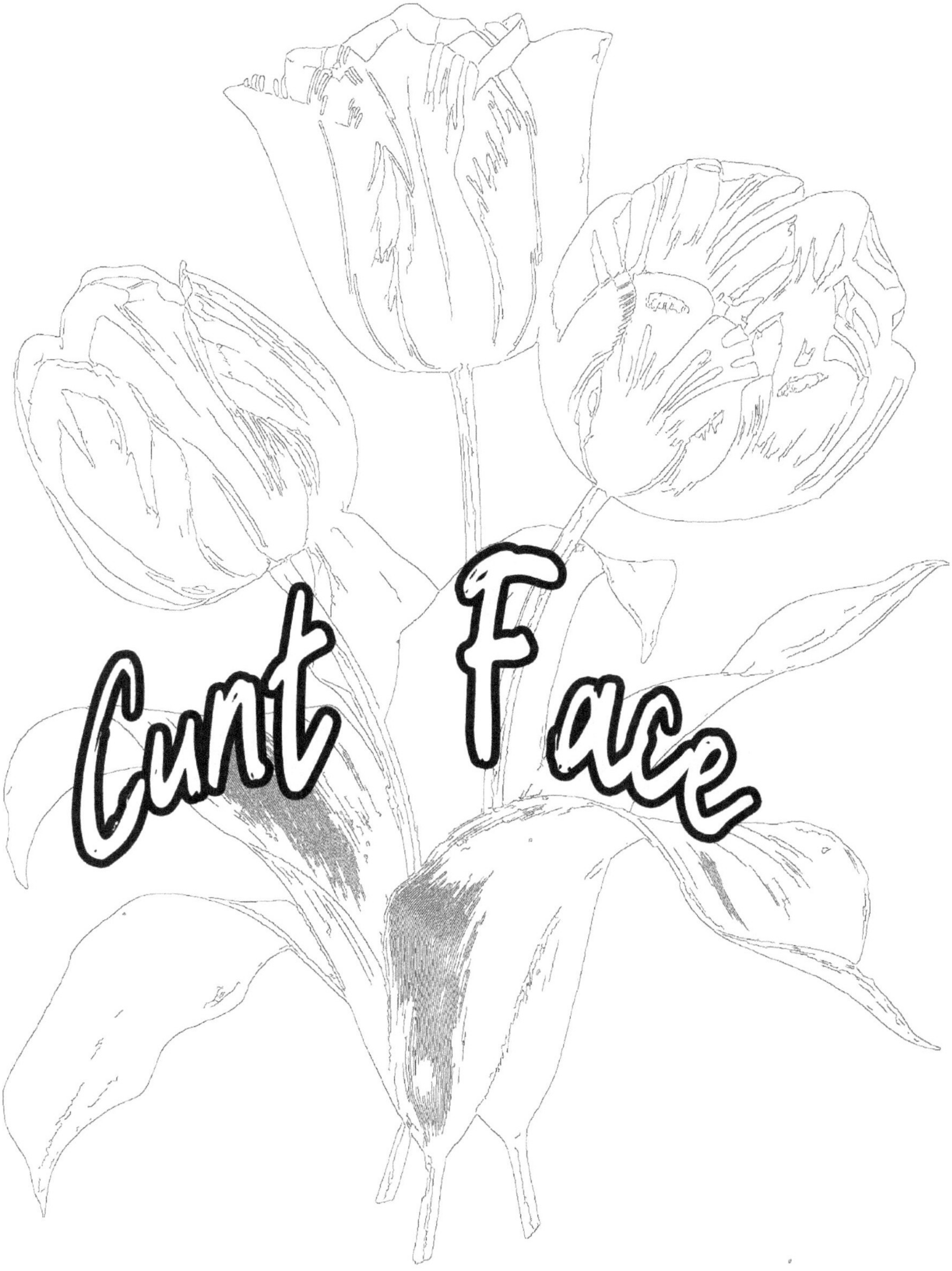
Cunt Face

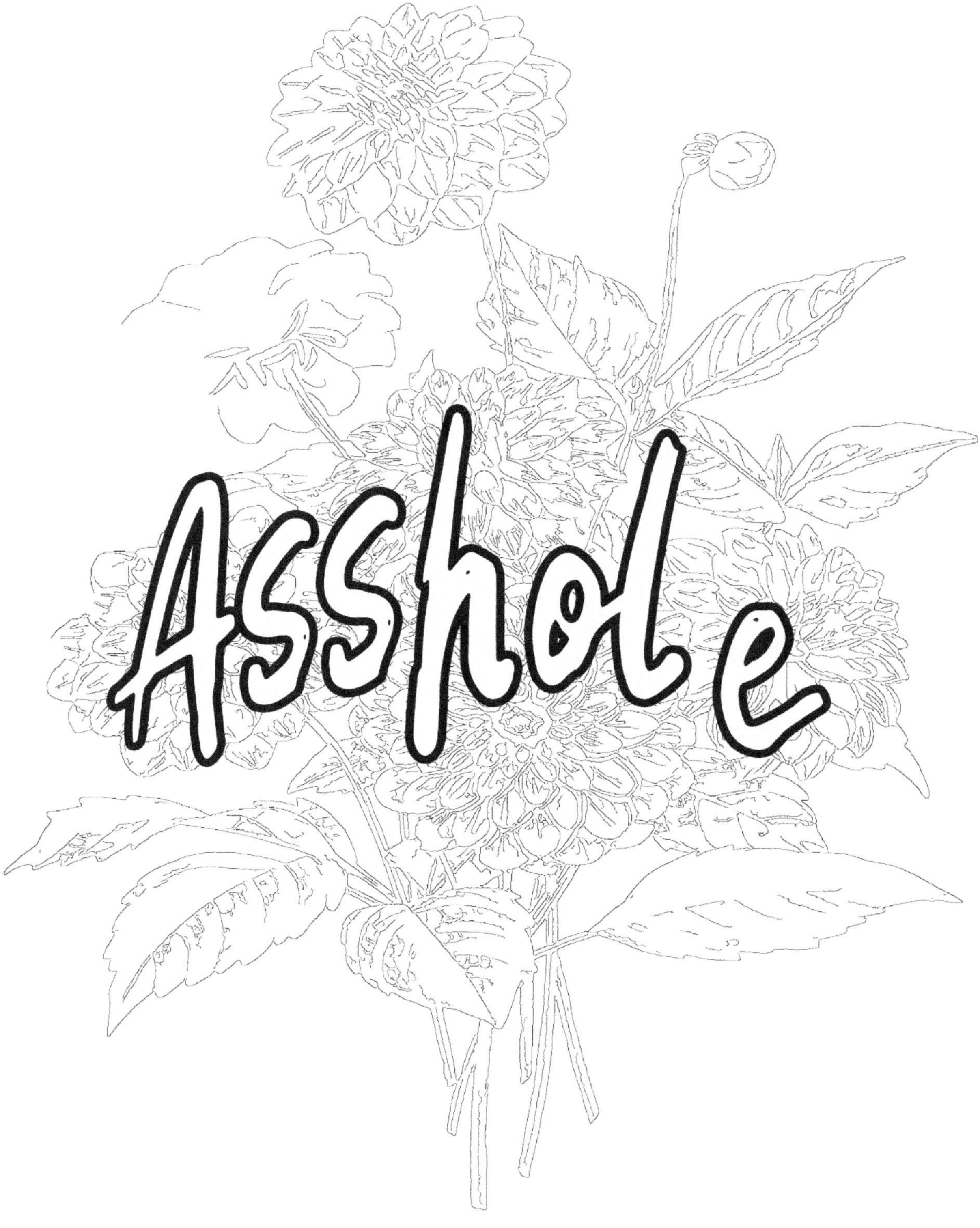
Asshole

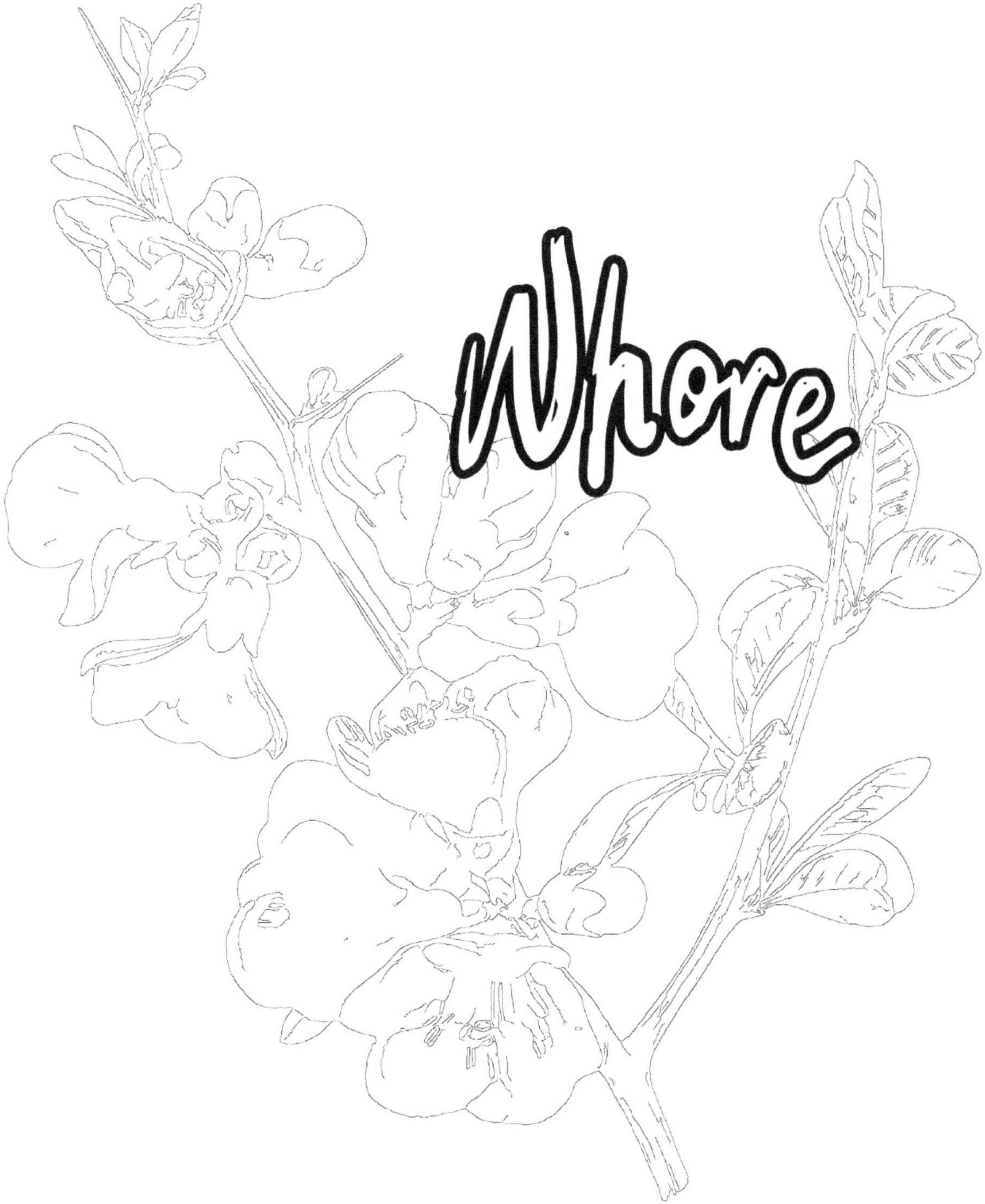
Whore

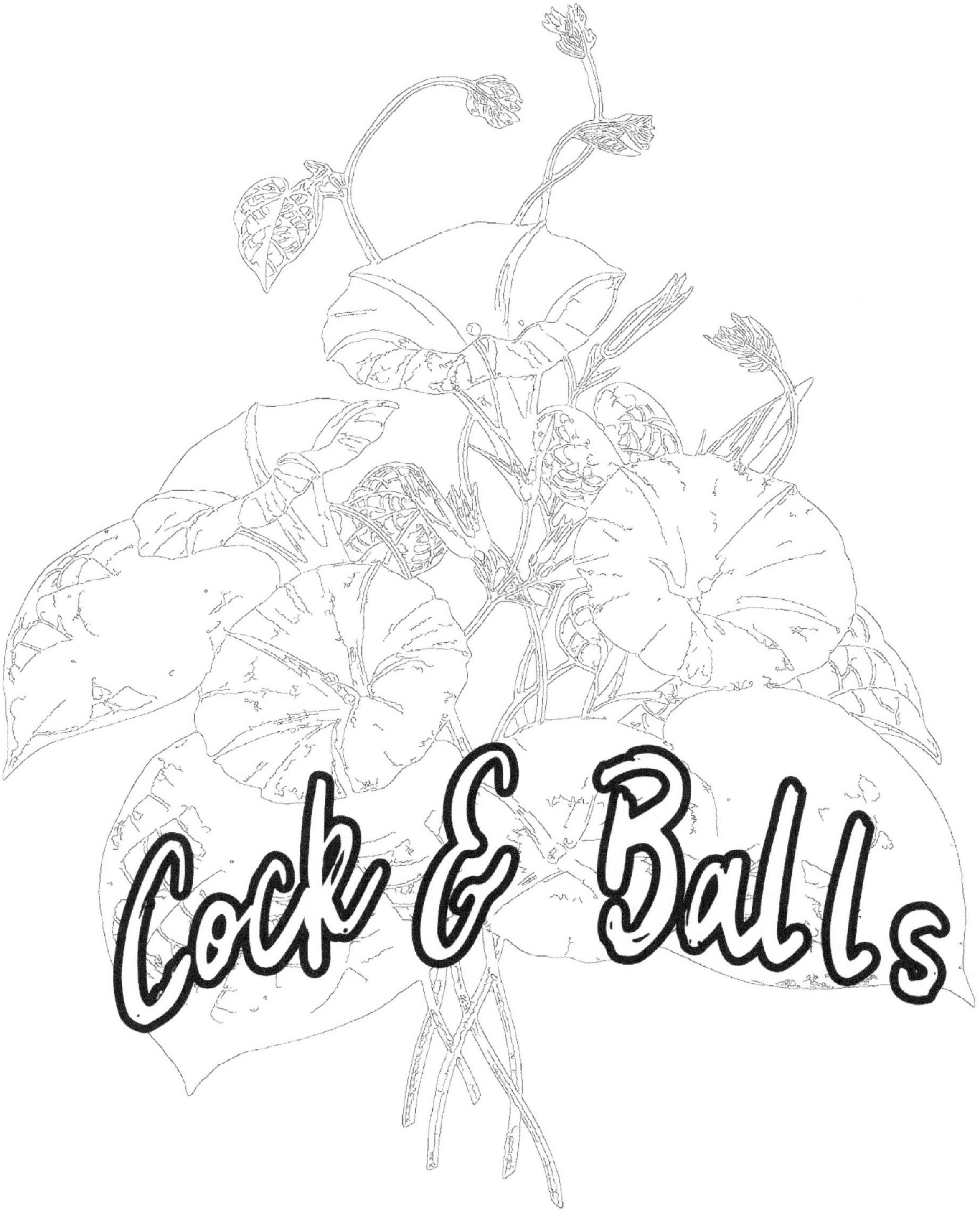
Cock & Balls

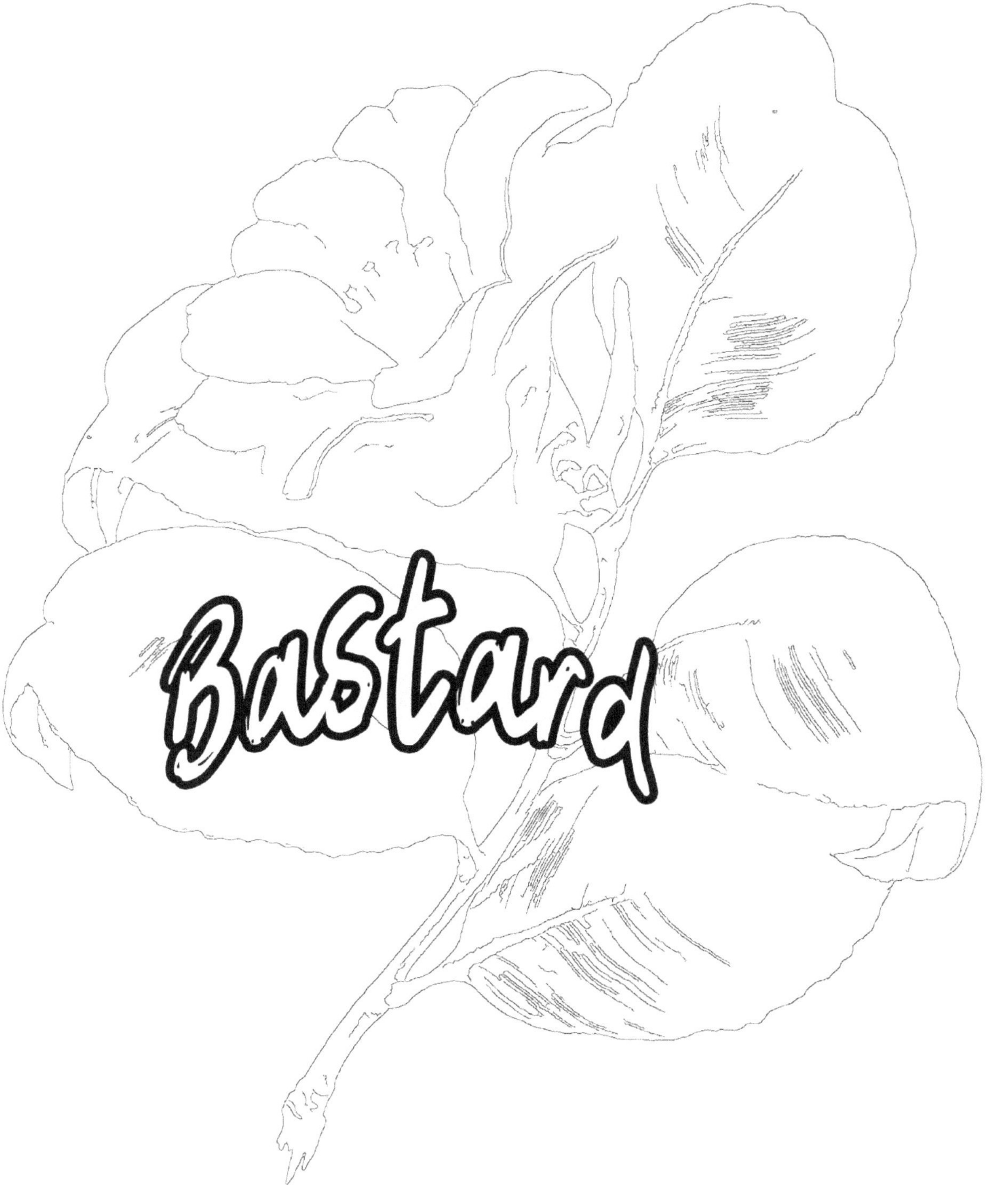
Bastard

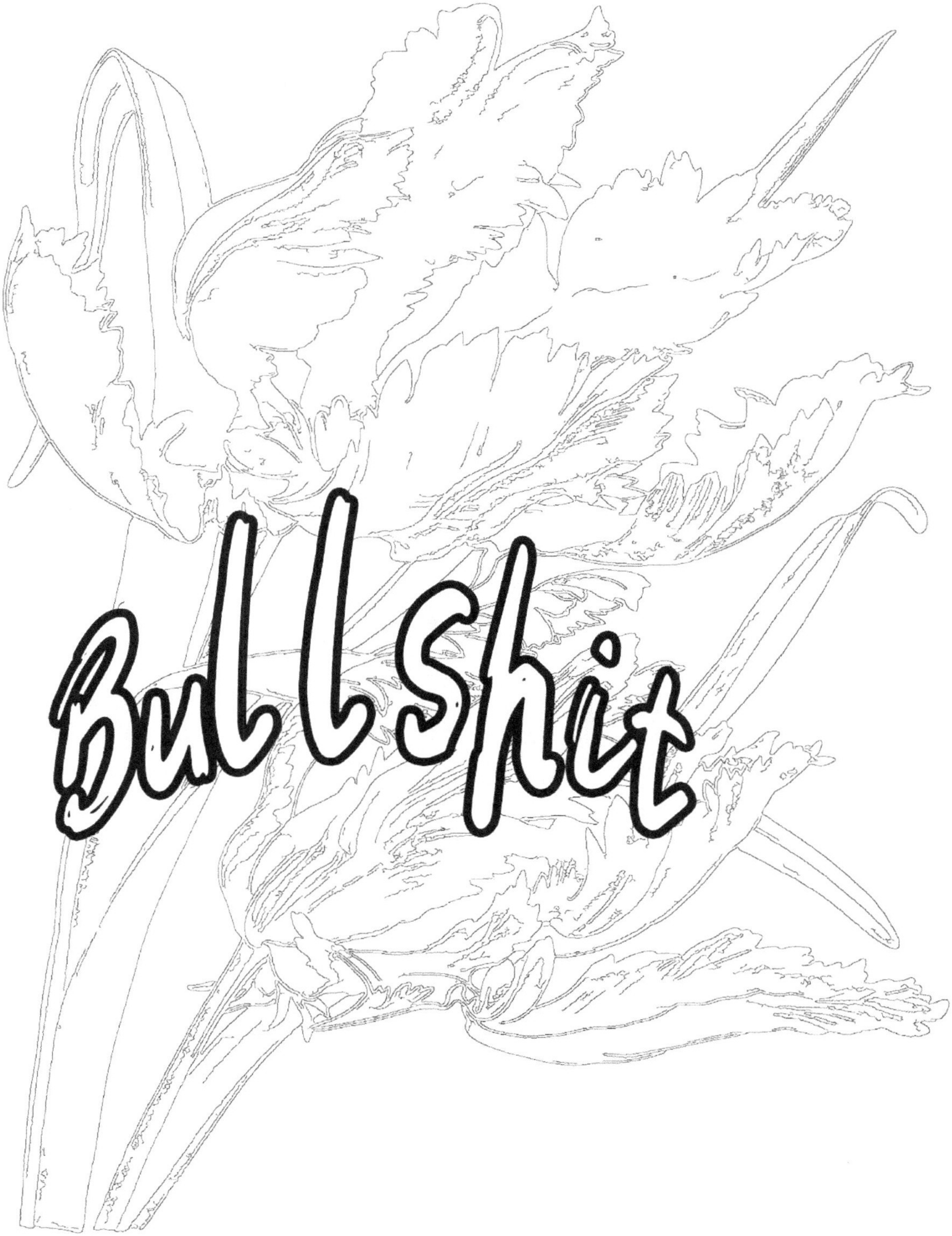
BullShit

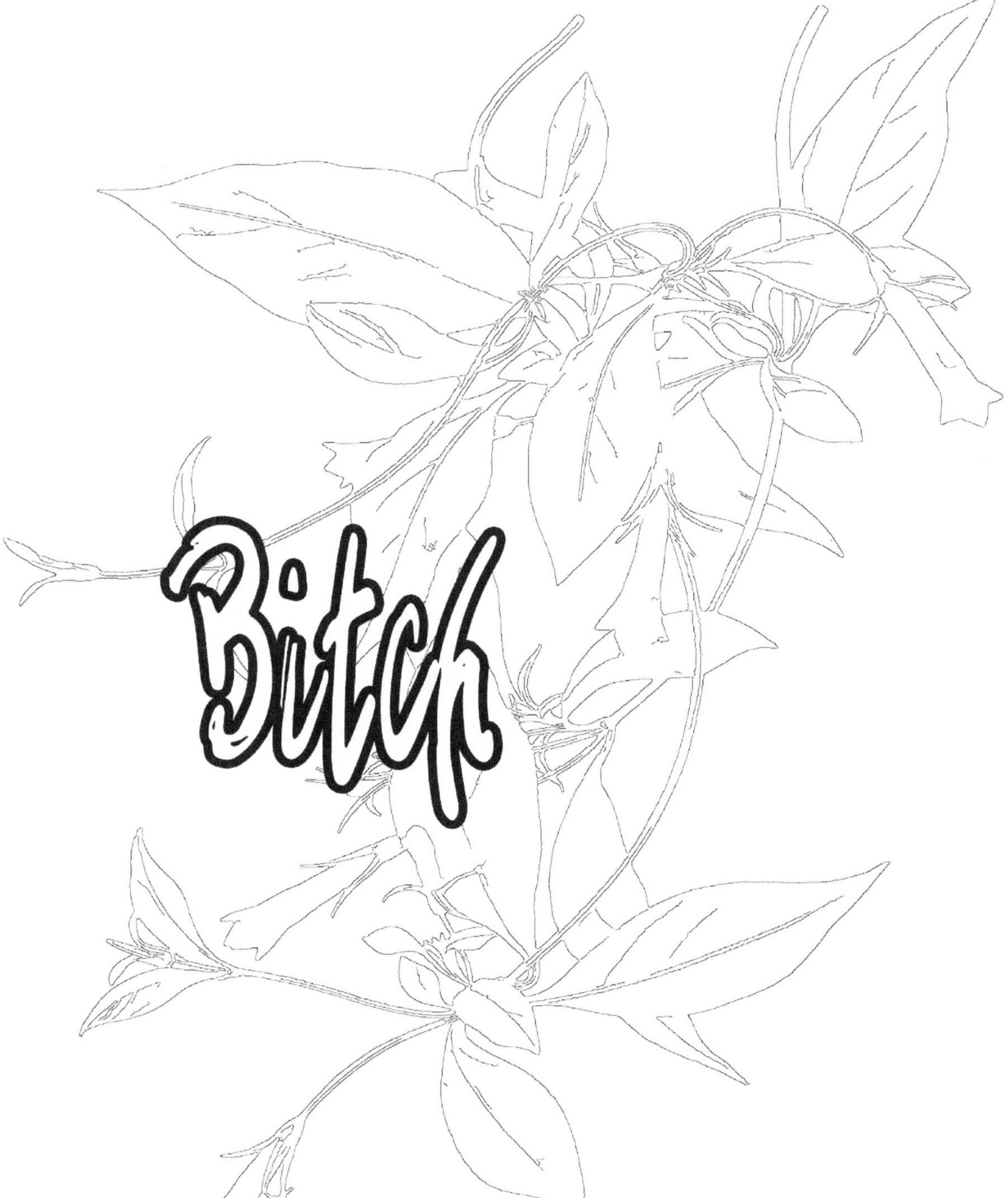
Bitch

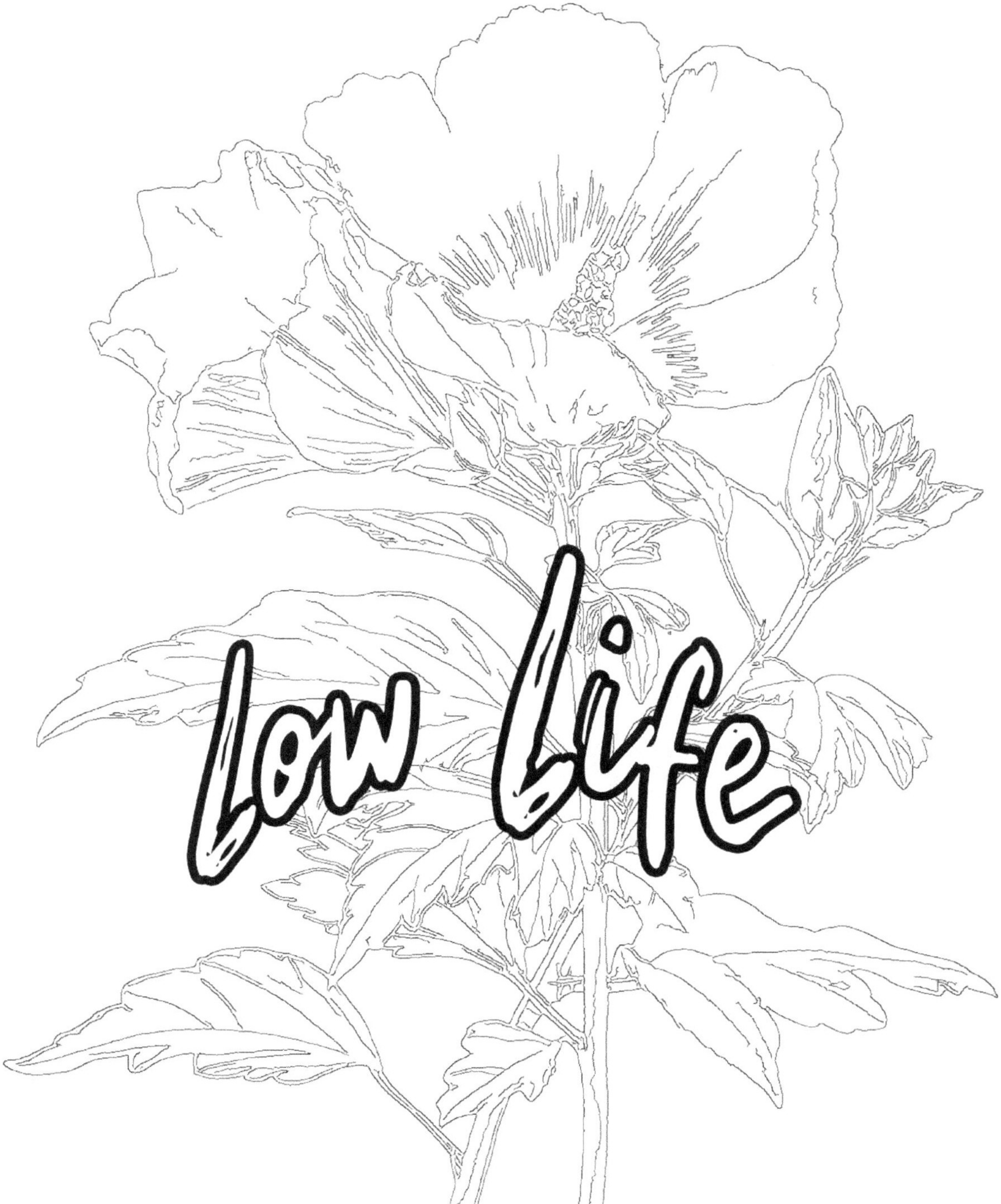
low life

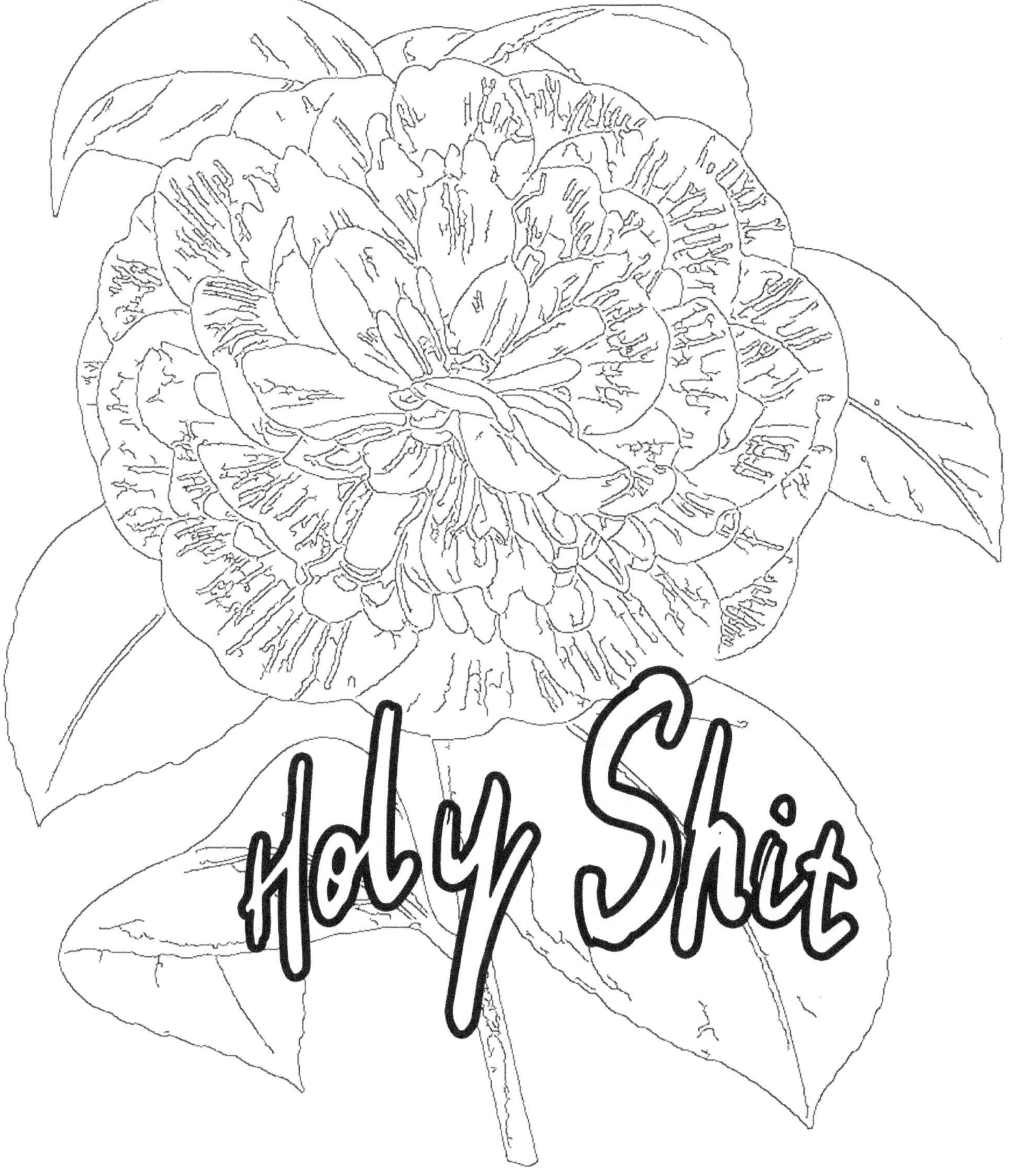
Holy Shit

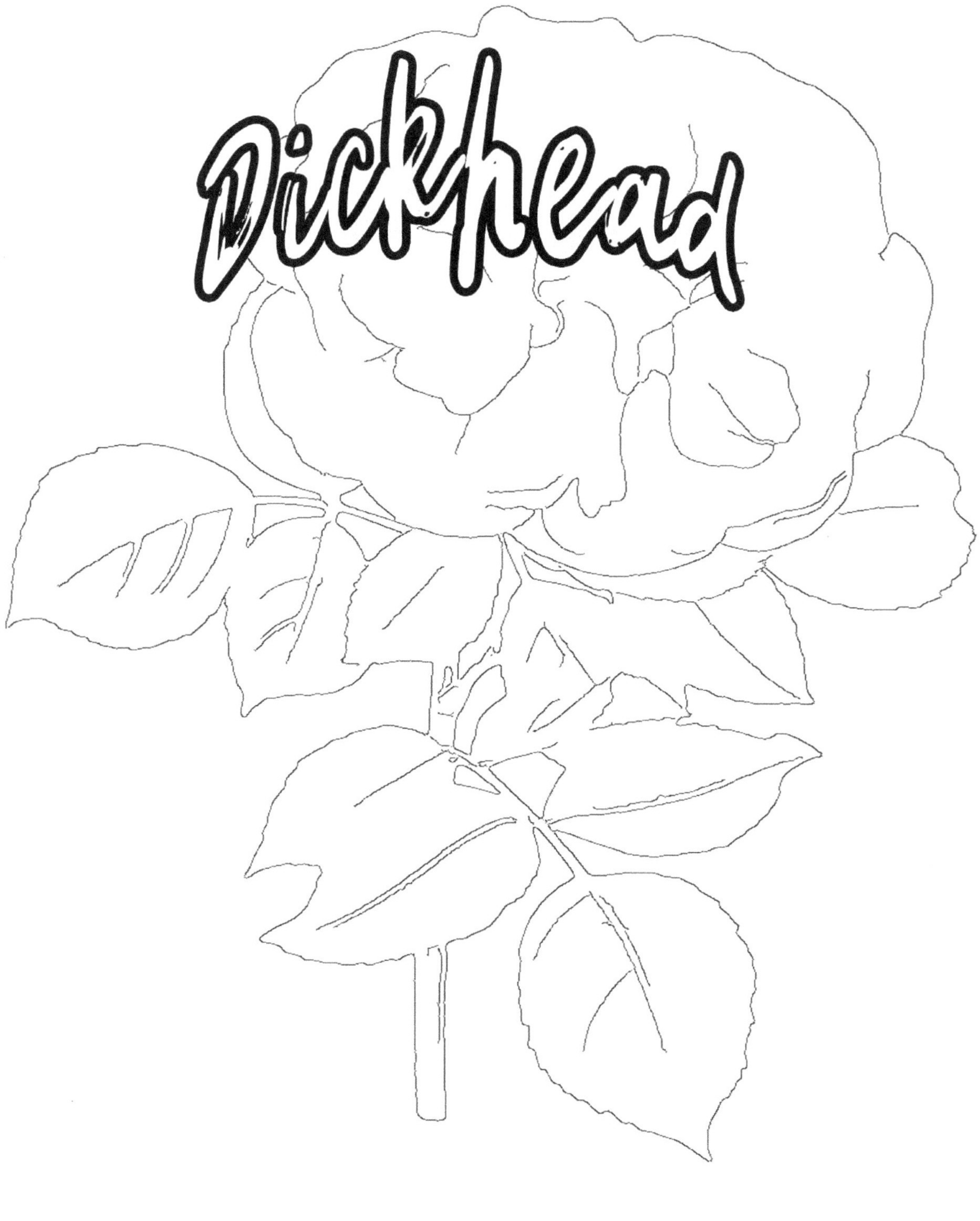
Dickhead

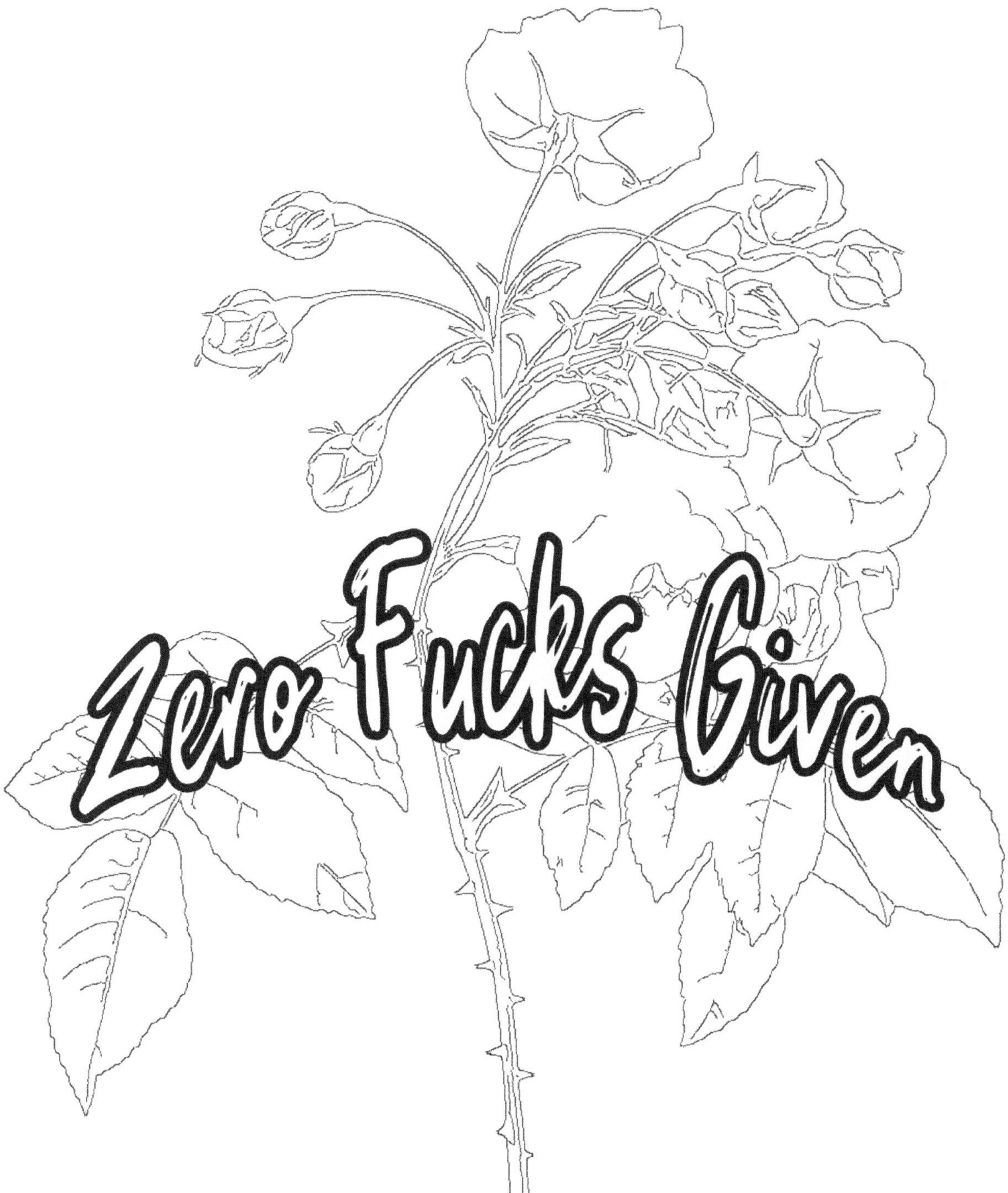
Zero Fucks Given

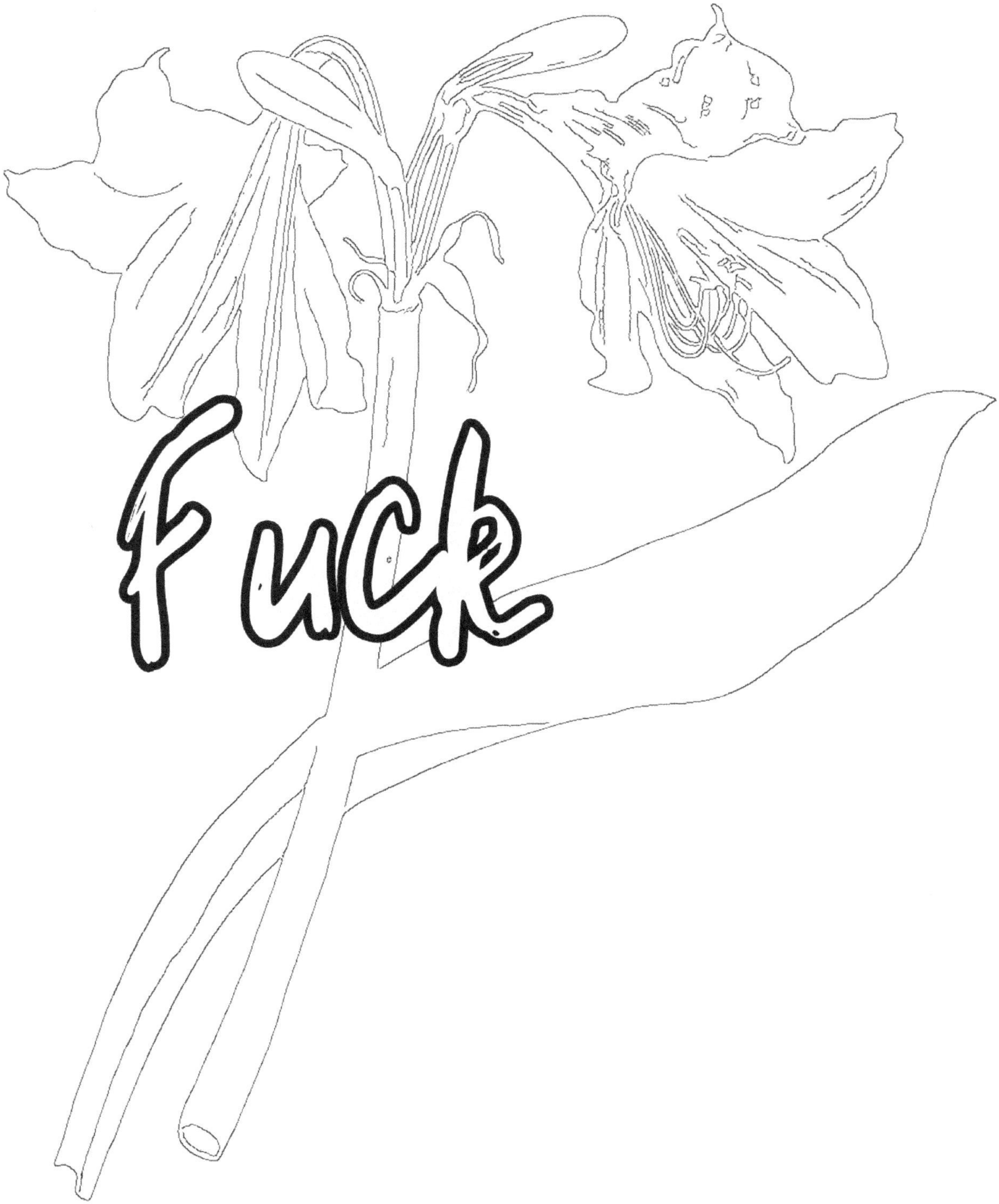
Fuck

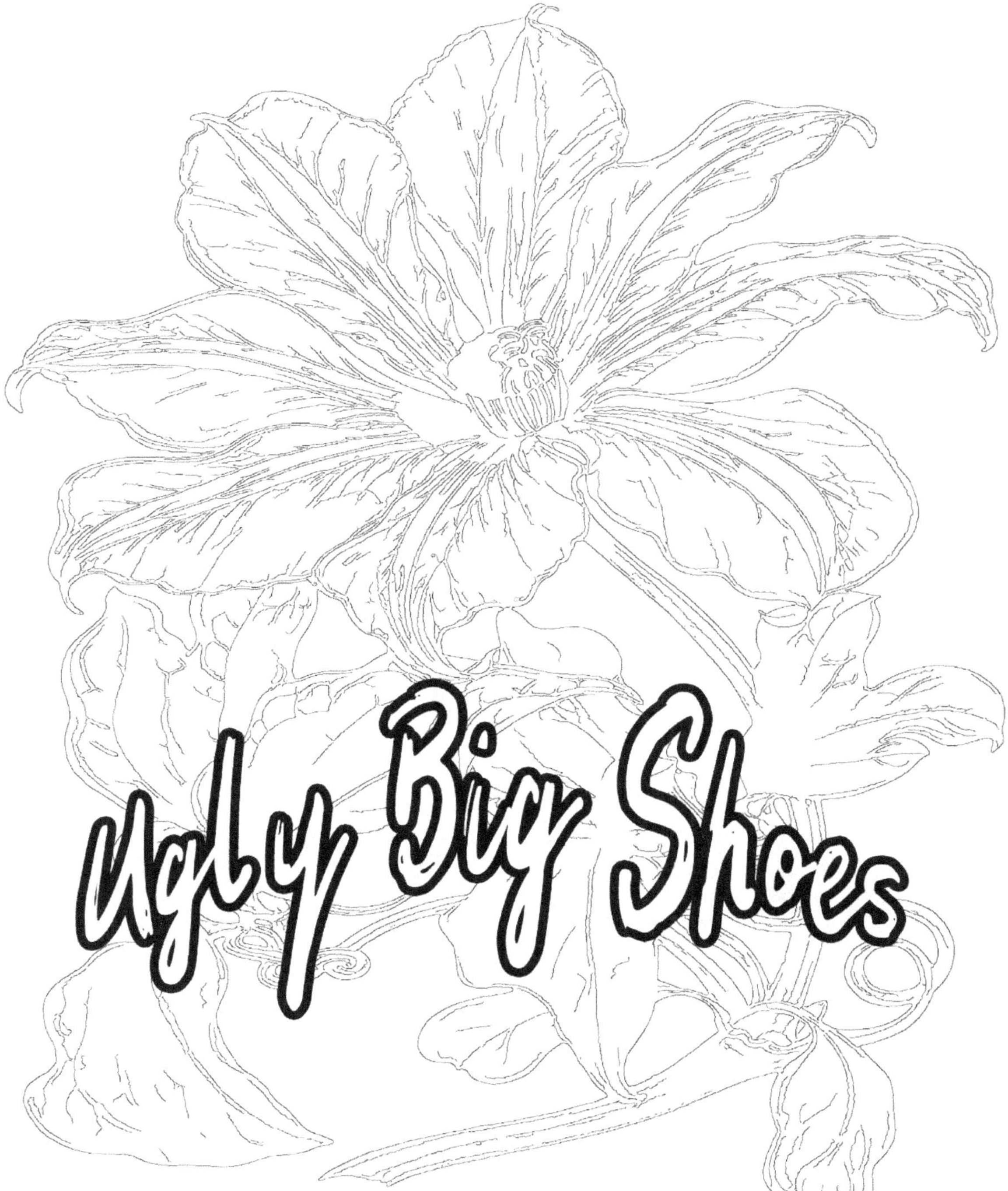
Ugly Big Shoes

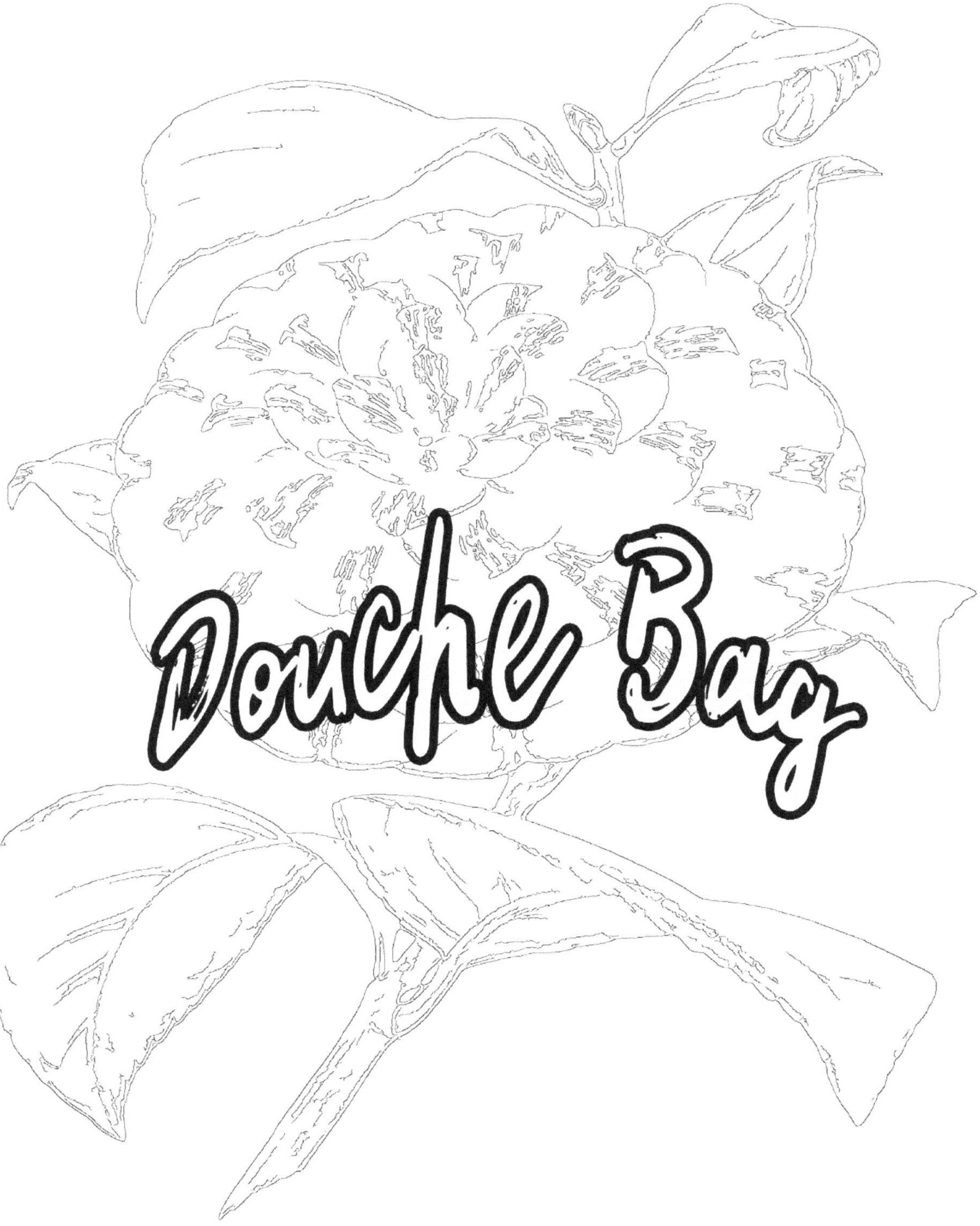
Douche Bag

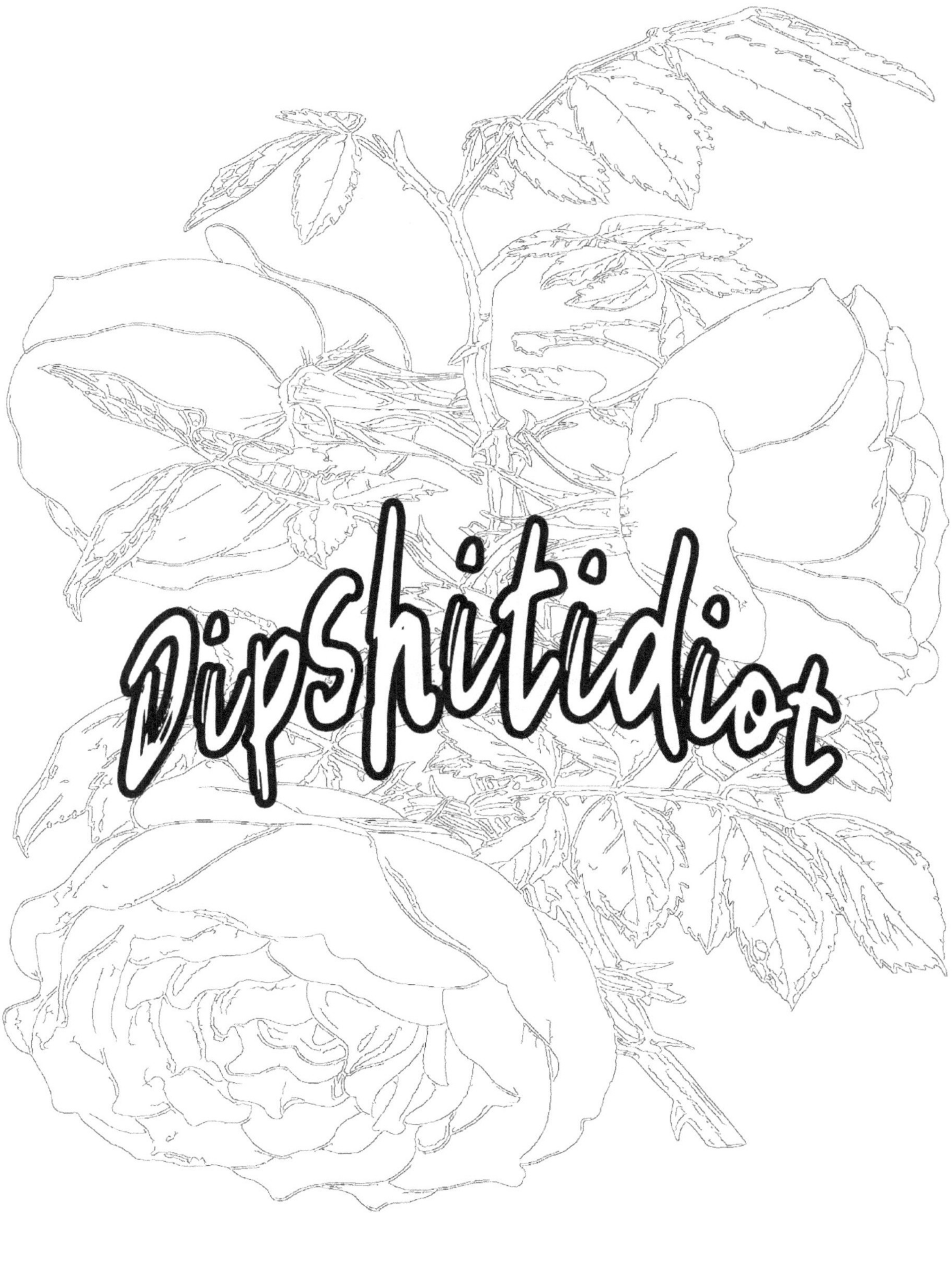
DipShitidiot

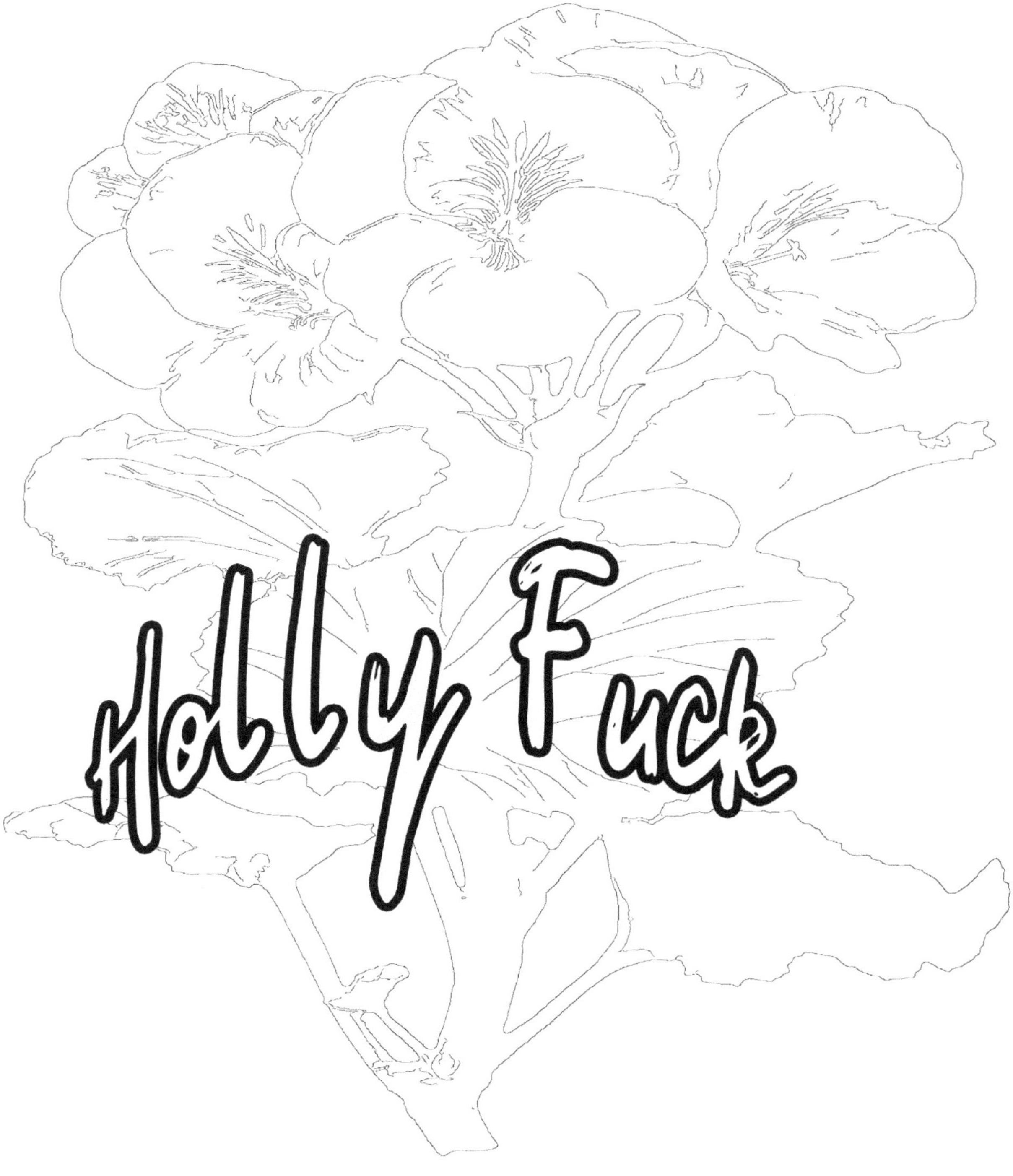
Holly Fuck

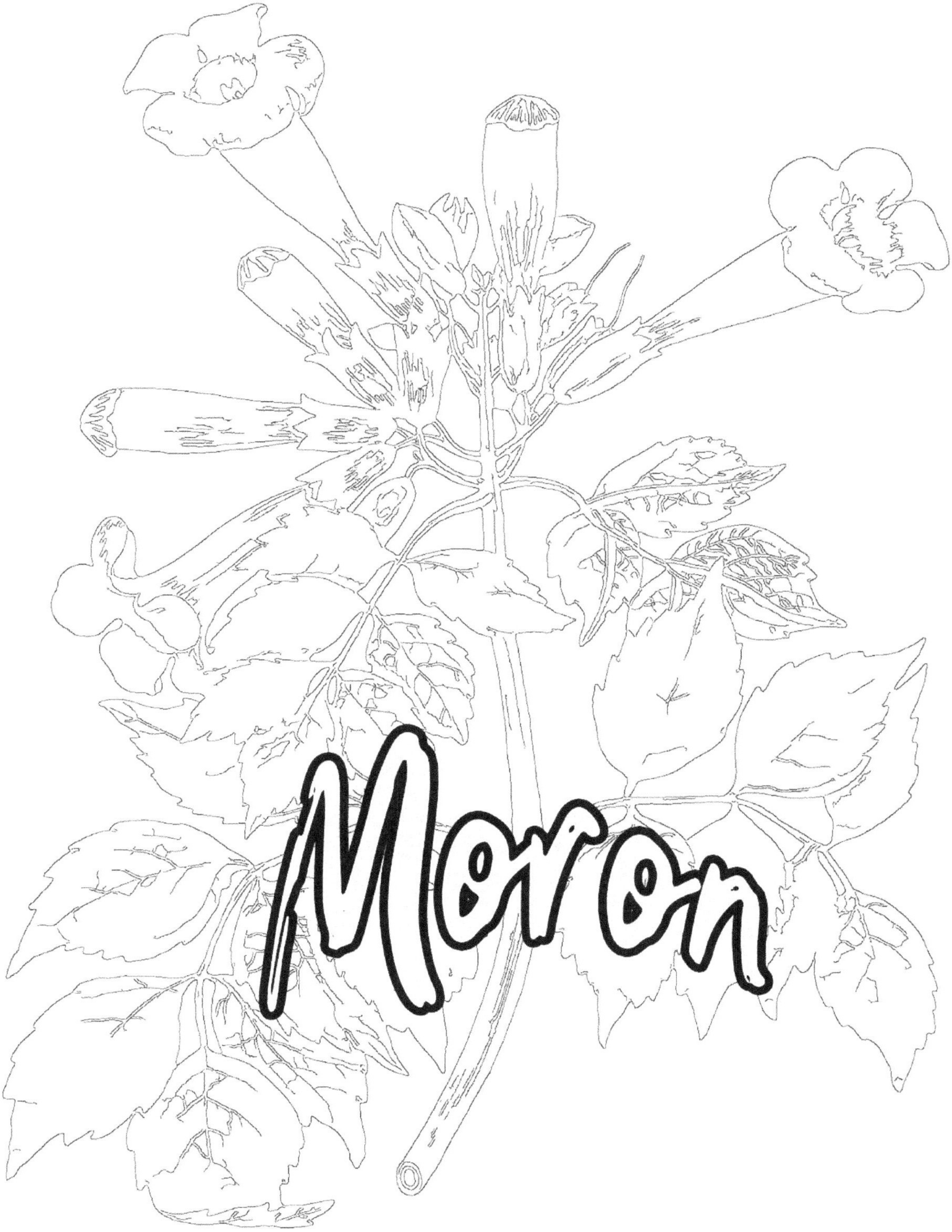
Moron

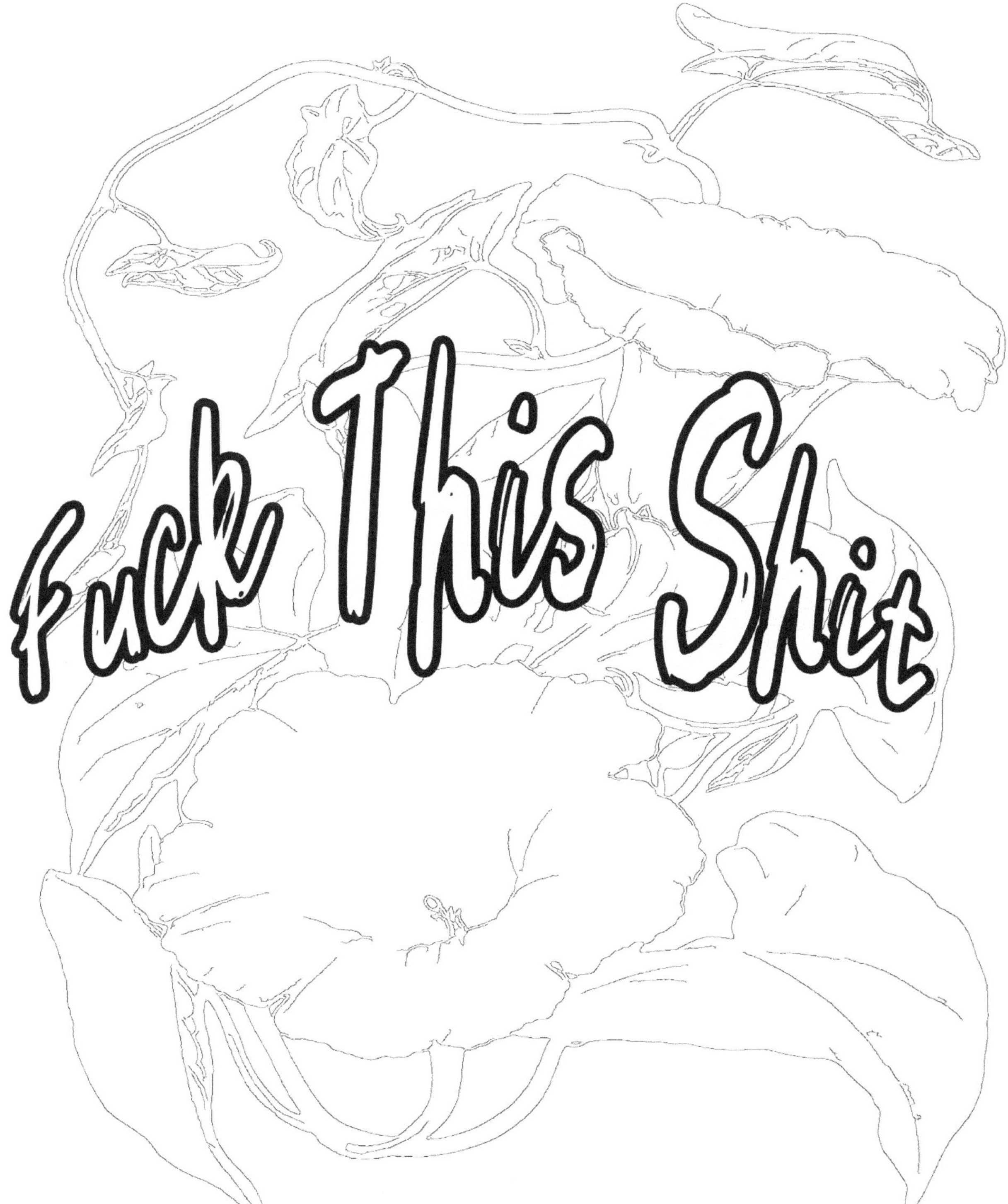
Fuck This Shit

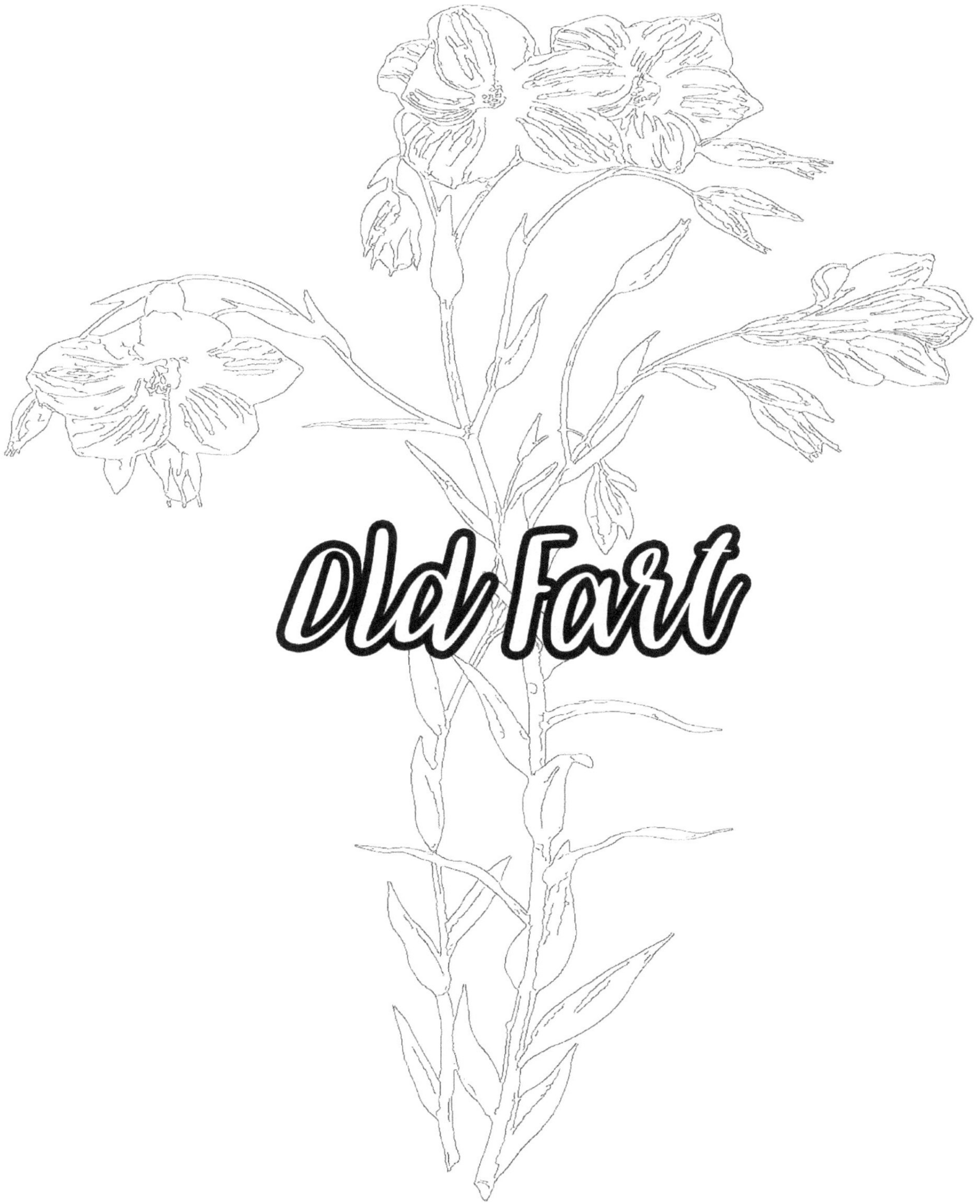
Old Fart

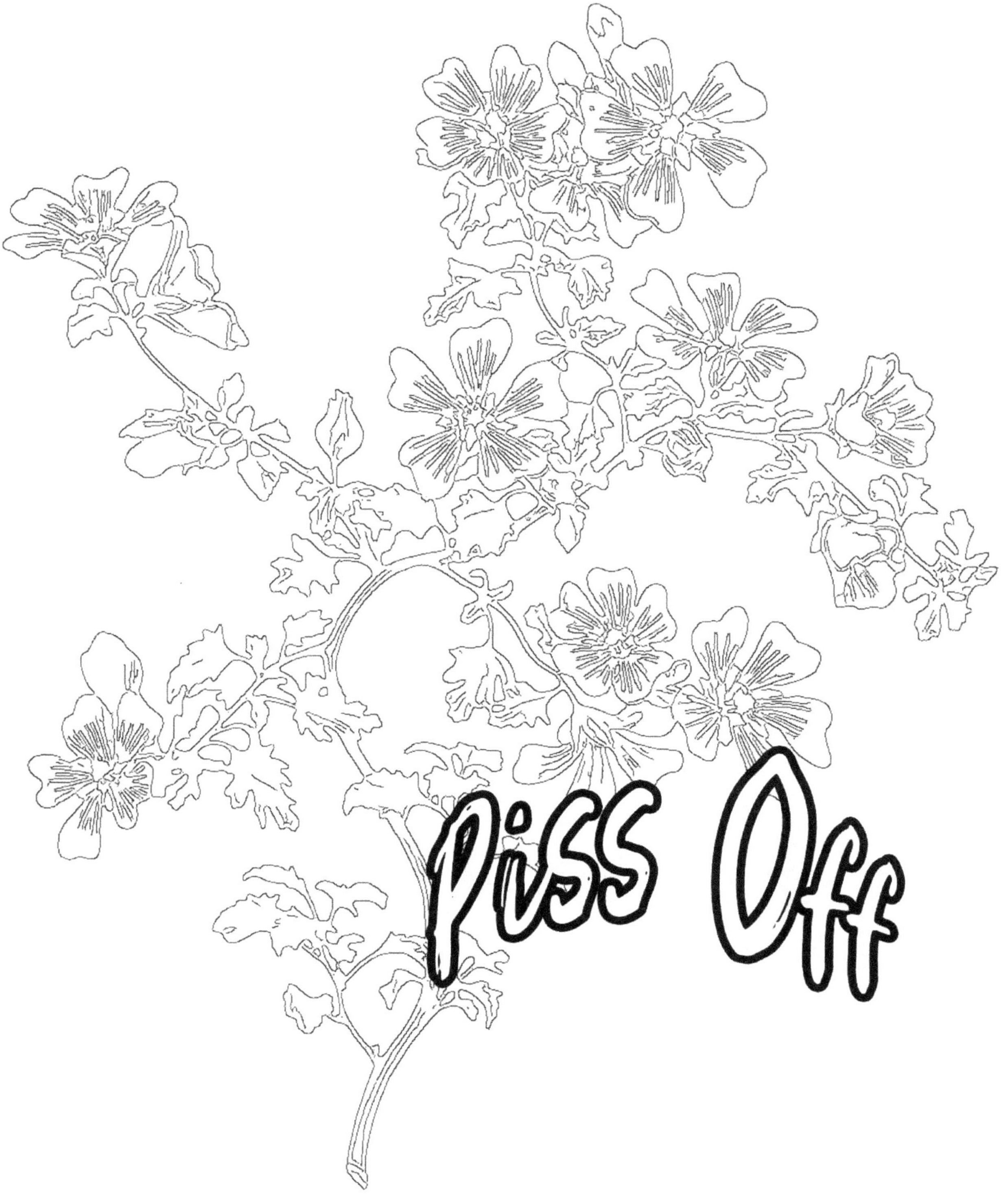
Piss Off

Have a good day.

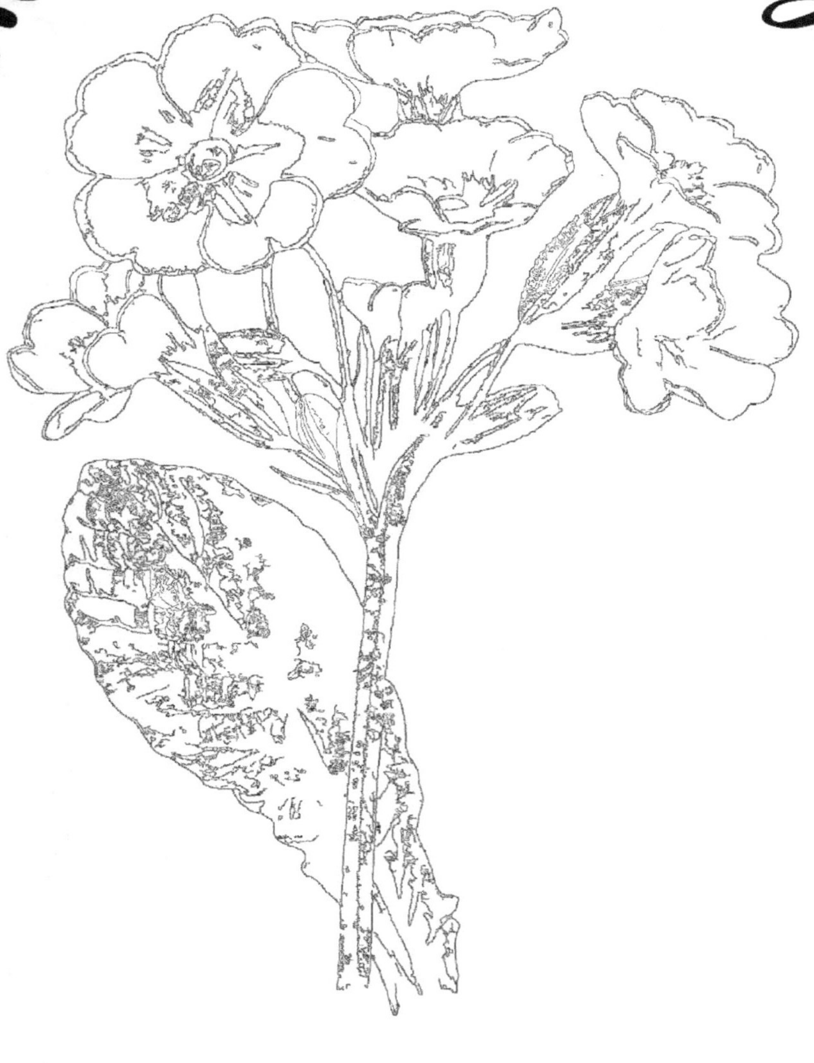

www.ingramcontent.com/pod-product-compliance
Lightning Source LLC
Chambersburg PA
CBHW081618220526
45468CB00010B/2935
9781983670220